UNCOMFORTABLE
grace

Uncomfortable Grace
by Marsha Thompson

Copyright © 2020 Marsha Thompson.

ISBN-13: 978-1735028415

Published by Lazarus Tribe Media, LLC
Rome, Georgia, USA
www.lazarustribe.media

Art by Sandra Auger

Edited by Rachel Newman

UNCOMFORTABLE
grace

BY MARSHA THOMPSON

Lazarus Tribe Media
Rome, Georgia

Dedicated to Caleb, Eli, & Sydney
All proceeds go to Cumberland Wilderness Retreat
www.cumberlandwilderness.org

Thank you...
Keith for your love and support
*Rachel Newman at Lazarus Tribe Media
for helping me share my heart*
Sandra Auger for sharing your artistic talent with me
Carmen Wood for editing and helping me cross the finish line

Contents

"You see, all of us, every day, demonstrate again and again that we need God to continue to work on us. God loves you too much to leave you unfinished. He cares for you too much to leave you undone,

so He comes to you with

uncomfortable grace.

Sure, you and I want the grace of relief. The grace of release and relief will come someday. But what we really now need is the

grace of refinement.

Are there places where you're crying for the grace of God, and you're not realizing that you're getting it? But it's not the grace of release, and it's not the grace of relief.

It's the boiling

grace of personal transformation.

You see, God will take you where you do not want to go in order to produce in you what you could not achieve on your own. In those unexpected moments, don't run away from your Lord; run to him. You are not being forsaken; you are being loved."

- Paul David Tripp

Foreword

Heartwork. It is a road that anyone can walk as they journey through life. Although many choose the path to explore their own heart, it still remains the road less traveled. Marsha is one who chose to slow down in the midst of her shame and disappointment with herself and begin the hard work of exploring her own heart. She hoped that it might lead her to understanding the reasons for her choices and behaviors that were slowly destroying her.

It has been an arduous journey, as heartwork usually is, but as anyone knows who has bolstered their courage to embark on their own journey of getting to know their heart, that person will never be the same. One never backs up from doing their heartwork. Rather, they typically want to help others find their way out of darkness, confusion, and emotional duress.

It is through this desire to help others bring light into

the dark places of their lives that Marsha and I connected. Soon after my husband, Nathan, and I founded Battlefield Ministries in June of 1996, the Lord clearly prompted me to "get what you do in the office out of the office." I responded to His prompt by saying, "Okay. I will do this, but I need You to surround me with some smart women who can pull it off."

The very next Sunday He led me to ask Marsha Thompson if she would be interested in helping me put together and lead a women's event. I was sure she would say no to this invitation because no American woman needs one more thing on her plate. But, she did not say no! She said, "I would be honored!" I couldn't believe it! So Marsha and I began meeting to develop and plan, "Come to the Water...and be set FREE!" This was the first of many more life-changing events for women, for families, for ourselves.

About a year before that first women's event, Nathan and I had walked Marsha and Keith through their pre-marital counseling. After marrying, they continued leading the thriving singles Bible study group which Keith had previously led alone. It soon became evident that these two were the Pied Piper for couples, and Marsha was a magnet for women. Their singles group evolved into a couples group, and has now extended to families as they host family camps (as well as other events) at their camp, Cumberland Wilderness Retreat.

Marsha is a leader.

And, as you will read, Marsha was hurting.

For many of us, our internal struggles are covered; covered by the known and the unknown that has created shame in our lives; covered by our ability to perform and our desire to be well thought of by those around us. While this may be true, some of us find the courage, in the

Lord's strength, to go toward those unseen deeper matters of our heart. Marsha is a great example of going toward and embracing the journey needed to identify and tend to those deeper, tougher matters in order to get to those clean, clear places. It's an encouraging footnote to share that over the years, Nathan and I have watched God powerfully use Marsha even before her knowledge that this significant heartwork was necessary. In and through all of this, she operated in what she knew, and He has used her all along. Now, after doing this work, she recognizes not only that God uses her but she is able to receive the joy that comes from being His vessel.

It is our hope that you be one of those who pay attention to your own heart as you wander through this "heart laid open" journey that Marsha shares so bravely. And may we all live in the action of love that is not only slow to cast a stone, but makes way for us to be impacted by the realities we all face that would serve to set themselves up against the gifting that lies within each of us.

Jane Phillips, Co-founder, Battlefield Ministries, Inc.

Rome, Georgia, August 2020

1.

My Story

*I*n the summer of 2017, I was struggling with coming to terms with the fact that I was turning forty-three years old. My mom was forty-three when she died. Searching for the significance of this year, I scribbled "P. S.", for Patti Sue, on a piece of paper. Adjacent to it, I wrote "43." Because of the resemblance of the note to Psalm 43, I thumbed through my Bible to find the passage.

> *"Vindicate me, my God, and plead my cause against an unfaithful nation. Rescue me from those who are deceitful and wicked. You are God my stronghold. Why have you rejected me? Why must I go about mourning, oppressed by the enemy? Send me your light and your faithful care, let them lead me; let them bring me*

> *to your holy mountain, to the place where you*
> *dwell. Then I will go to the altar of God, to God,*
> *my joy and my delight. I will praise you with*
> *the lyre, O God, my God. Why, my soul, are you*
> *downcast? Why so disturbed within me? Put*
> *your hope in God, for I will yet praise him, my*
> *Savior and my God." Psalm 43:1-5 (NIV)*

This Psalm is relaying the story of David's divided heart. God is his refuge, and yet he feels forsaken. Sometimes, we can feel forgotten and unloved by God because of the pain we have experienced, or our unanswered prayers. But, He has not left us. We have to pray for spiritual light to see the Truth. We must confess our sins and allow God to fill our brokenness. Life is a battle we must fight by hiding the Word in our hearts and pressing on towards the goal. This is hard to do, but it is necessary if we want an abundant, joyful life. It has taken most of my lifetime to learn this truth. Here is some of my story of how the Lord has revealed His grace to me.

Mom

I was born in Birmingham, Alabama, to Bill (William) and Patti Crow. My dad was a giant of a man, standing six feet eight inches tall and over three-hundred pounds. My mom, on the other hand, was only five feet five inches tall, but she had a giant personality. I had a good childhood despite the chaos. My parents divorced when I was a toddler, and while my brother went to live with my dad, I stayed with my mom. We had visits every other weekend. After the divorce, my mom remarried three times. The first two guys left much to be desired. She married her last husband, Gene, when I was in the third grade. They seemed to be really happy. I liked him, but it was hard to share my mom with another person. Despite these chaotic relationships, my mom always made me feel important and loved. She was my world.

My mom was an only child, and with her extremely overprotective parents, she could not wait to get out of the house. Her exploration of the world only led to a lot of disappointment and heartache. Thankfully, her parents, Ralph and Avis, were always there for her. She was a "daddy's girl," and she loved helping him at their gas station and grocery store in Rockledge, Alabama. They were well known and loved by their community. My mom and I moved back to that small town when I was in the first grade to be close to them. I would go visit them by taking the trail through the woods that connected our houses. My grandmother always had the perfect snack when I got home from school. It seems really odd now, but I looked forward to having mashed potatoes, a half-frozen Pepsi, or a Little Debbie cake waiting for me when I got off the bus.

My grandparents' store holds so many precious memories.

As you can tell in this photo, my mom was quite the "daddy's girl."

When I was in the eighth grade, my grandmother died from heart failure. My granddad followed a mere two weeks later. He had an abdominal aneurysm, but according to the doctors, it is likely that he grieved himself to death. My mom lost both of her parents within a few weeks' time, and the loss left her heartbroken. I was thankful she had my stepdad to comfort her. Though my family was devastated, we somehow pulled through.

This is my favorite photo of my grandparents.

Dad

As a result of my parents' divorce, my dad went to live with his mom, Romilda. The divorce was very hard on him, and living with her was a big help as he transitioned into being a single dad to my brother, Barry. My grandmother had a beautiful home on top of the mountain in Smokerise, Alabama. I loved visiting them twice a month. She always made everything so special. She took care of my dad and brother, instilling that same nurturing quality in me.

In addition to the stress of becoming a single dad, my dad's health began to fail. He had the first of three heart attacks when I was in elementary school. A few years later, my grandmother's health began to decline also. When I was in the ninth grade, she passed away, leaving my father alone to take care of my brother. It was hard watching my grandmother's home lose the life that carried my best childhood memories. The fact that my dad did not have his mom made me feel like it was my responsibility to make sure he was okay. When I would visit, I cleaned the house and made his lunches for the week. He did not expect me to do this. I felt bad that he was alone, and I worried about his health. He was a great "little girl" daddy, and during my visits with him, he always took the time to play with me. One of our favorite activities was going shopping. He would help me put together the perfect outfit. However, by the time I was in my teenage years, I felt more like a caretaker than a daughter.

My parent's wedding with their parents on each side.

*My Grandmother and me at her retirement party. She was
a librarian at the Princeton Baptist Medical Center.*

My brother Barry, cousin Mark, and me with our grandmother.

*My grandmother loved to take photos of us on her back
deck. The second photo included my cousin, Mark.*

Balancing two different lives, one with my mom and
one with my dad, had its consequences. I see now that my
parents dealt with insecurities, many of which I took on
as well. I felt inadequate in comparison to others because
of my family's brokenness. I also struggled in school, and
my mom worked a lot, so she could not provide the help
I needed. I knew my parents and grandparents loved me
dearly, but they were not Christians. They ultimately could
not point me to the true Source of security and identity
that I needed growing up.

As my sophomore year of high school began, my mom
and Gene started having marital problems. They were getting counseling, and though it was apparent that they both
had issues, she assured me that they were working through
them. One day that year, my mom unexpectedly called the
school and told me to ride home with my friend, Tonya. My mom was waiting for me when I got off the bus
at Tonya's house, and she explained that my stepdad had
committed suicide in our home that day. Confusion overwhelmed me, and I could not grasp what had happened. In
the midst of that immense confusion, I was not concerned

with my own grief. I was overcome with worry about what others would think of us.

Gene's death had a dramatic impact on me, and I am so thankful the Lord placed people in my life to help me during this time. My childhood friends, Tonya and Christy, along with their parents, provided encouragement and stability in my life. My teachers at Sardis High School were also very supportive. Lisa Hicks, my P.E. teacher and track coach, had a significant impact on my life. Her influence inspired me to become a P.E. teacher and coach just like her.

After so many losses, my family was predictably fragile. I saw my mom hurt and broken, and though it was incredibly difficult to watch, that brokenness was what ultimately led her to the Lord. In a special letter she wrote to me, she encouraged me to seek the Lord as well. She expressed her hope that I would invest in my relationship with Him, and she even suggested I quit my job so that I would have more time to get involved in my church youth group.

I still have this letter because of its importance to my journey of finding Christ.

(2) in this world (yes, another sermon)
Life is sometimes very bumpy and filled with problems. If your faith is strong, you can cope much better with any problems that comforts you.

I would have had a nervous break down if I did not have faith in God. It is so comforting to know that he watches over us and keeps us from harm. He is our survival kit.

There is much more security in trusting God then there is in anything else (money, friends etc.)

You need to decide if you might want to quit your job since you will be going on more retreats at church.

My mom also prompted me to go on a youth trip that changed my life forever. While on this trip, Amanda Faucett, a dear friend of mine, led a devotion explaining how God is the light, and we live in darkness until we ask Him to be the Lord of our lives. I wanted to be a light shining on a hill, but I had no light of my own. That simple idea broke me. In my brokenness, I confessed my sin and asked God to shine His light through me. When He opened my eyes, I experienced peace and hope for the first time! I wanted to share Jesus with everyone, even though I was immature in my faith, and I still had a lot to learn. God had only begun to make sense of the utter chaos I had lived in for most of my life. I joined First Baptist Church of Boaz, Alabama, where Aaron Johnson was the youth pastor. He was a great teacher and a lot of fun. He and his wife Denise have always been there for me.

The following year was my junior year of high school, and college was appearing right over the horizon like a beautifully unknown cloud of new experiences. To add to this hope, I was pleased to find out that my mom and dad, who had remained friends, began dating again. I was thankful that they had reconnected. In my mind, they could now take care of each other. Their relationship continued to strengthen, and they planned to remarry the next year.

However, those plans would never be realized. The Bible says in Proverbs 16:9,

> *"The heart of a man plans his way, but the Lord establishes his steps."*

This was true in the lives of my parents. The plans they had to remarry did not come to fruition. In January of 1991, in my junior year of high school, my mom had a brain aneurysm. After spending two weeks in the hospital, she passed away.

My parents and my brother.

One of the few photos I have with my mom.

I felt absolutely lost and alone. My closest source of security and comfort was gone. Although my dad and brother eventually moved in with me, life was incredibly sad. It was hard for me to go out with friends because I knew my dad was mourning the love of his life. Special occasions were even worse, and I dreaded holidays. I could not even watch a movie without being reminded of what I had lost. Because I had to grow up so quickly, I was not able to relate to my peers anymore, either. Small things like yelling out from the shower for my mom to bring me a towel caused me to go to bed crying and wake up crying. I was living with seemingly endless pain crushing my heart, yet I learned to dry it up, and put on a smile. I did not want anyone to feel sorry for me.

My mom's letter of encouragement included her desire for me to get involved at church. This turned out to be great advice. Aaron, my church family, and Jamie Faucett were great supports during this time. My best friend, Meca, and my classmates at school did all they could to encourage me. They voted me class president, homecoming queen, and prom queen. I was genuinely grateful...but still... empty and sad.

Another misfortune came when my dad had his second heart attack my senior year. Thankfully, he was able to recover from it, and we continued to try and live our lives. However, I was still numb from my mom's death. I had gotten used to expecting the worst since I had lost a loved one every year since the eighth grade.

Aaron and Denise at my senior prom.

I was crowned Homecoming Queen.

Me with Amanda (left) and Jamie (right).

Growing Up

High school graduation came and went. For my first semester of college, I chose to stick close to home and attend the local junior college. I also wanted to help my brother and his girlfriend, Odessa, as they were expecting a baby. Nate was my brother's first and only child, and this precious gift brought healing to our family. My dad adored Nate and kept him a lot. I can only imagine how my mom would have spoiled him if she had been there.

My dad and Nate.

After one semester at the junior college, I transferred to Jacksonville State University (JSU) in Jacksonville, Alabama. My Uncle Frank lived in Jacksonville and he allowed me to live in one of his apartments behind his car lot. He and my mom were really close. His son, Del, and the mechanic at the car lot, Raymond, were always there for me.

My cousin Del and me at the car lot.

Soon, I got involved at Baptist Campus Ministries (BCM) at Jacksonville State and grew tremendously in my faith. I felt like a bird that had been released from her cage. The most significant aspect of my new freedom was that I began to grow spiritually. Through the discipleship program at BCM, I went through the workbook, *Experiencing God,* by Henry and Richard Blackaby. I learned what it meant to have a relationship with the Lord. I became so passionate and thankful for this process that I soon became the discipleship director. I joined the Church of the Cross and was able to grow my relationship with the Lord even more.

During this time, I would check on my dad in Boaz, and occasionally take him to his cardiologist appointments in Birmingham. I worried about his health, and always felt terrible that he was alone. I tried to get him to attend church, but my efforts to persuade him to attend were futile. I believe that he had some insecurities about his size that created invisible barriers for him getting involved in a church. I was thankful that he had a few friends who would meet him for coffee at Wal-Mart regularly. These friends referred to him as the "gentle giant." Still, I was concerned about his salvation because I knew he did not know the Lord. He seemed to be under the impression that "good" people went to heaven. Looking back, I imagine my efforts to evangelize to him probably appeared pushy. I just wanted him to experience the peace that I had, and the hope of spending eternity in heaven.

Late one night, I got a call from my dad, and he said he was driving himself to the hospital in Boaz. Something was going on with his heart again. I hurried there, all the while, my past losses were telling me that he was not going to make it. When I got to the hospital, I saw the doctors working on my dad. It was like something in the movies. When the doctors came out, I had to talk to them alone. They prepared me for the worst and said that he needed more help than they could provide for him there. They soon transported him to Princeton Baptist Medical Center in Birmingham, Alabama, where he had his second open-heart surgery. Jamie and Meca drove me to the hospital in Birmingham that night. Meca stayed with me in the hospital hotel. Her presence was invaluable.

Thankfully, my dad survived the surgery but needed help recovering. He was in a lot of pain and was struggling with depression on top of it all. We decided it would be best if he moved into the tiny apartment I shared with Meca. I tried my best to take care of him, but I had many things going on in my life at that time. I was preparing my mom's house to go on the market, and renting out my grandparents' house. Both houses needed repairs. I am thankful to Joel, a church-college friend, for assisting Meca and me with the repairs on these houses. Without him, I would not have been able to handle all that was on my plate.

In the meantime, I found dad an apartment to live in. After a few weeks, he finally got strong enough to go home to his new place. After he left, I wrote him letters to remind him of how the Lord had given him a second chance in life.

Me with Joel and Meca.

After five long years, I finally graduated from JSU with a degree in Education. I received my first job at Coosa Middle School in Rome, Georgia. I taught P.E. and Health and coached basketball and track. I had no idea what I was doing, but I was ready to learn.

During my time at Coosa, I also got involved in The Church at Northside. I joined the singles' ministry and helped with the children's ministry program, AWANAs. It was here that I met Christy Slade, the wife of the AWANAs director. While working alongside her in the ministry, she told me that she had a feeling about who I was going to marry, and she predicted that it would likely happen the following year!

The mystery man's name was Keith Thompson. Christy told me that he was a physical therapist who had started his own clinic three years before. He had recently taken a leave of absence to do evangelism and discipleship work in East Africa. Ironically, Keith returned just as I was planning my first conference for singles. He became the leader of the singles when he returned, and we ended up spending a lot of time together planning events.

I think we both knew we were meant to be together,

but I was scared. Of course, this created some distance between us. In spite of that, one evening, Keith called and asked if he could come over to talk. He left his house in such a rush that he arrived with his shirt inside-out and backward. I thought that was really cute. He came to tell me that he believed we had a connection and wanted to know if we could move forward and go on a date. I said, "yes." About six months later, with the help of our friends, Jason Free and Isaac Phillips, he planned a romantic marriage proposal.

Isaac's parents were Nathan and Jane Phillips, two people for whom I am immensely grateful. I met them at The Church at Northside, where they were leading worship at the time. They founded Battlefield Ministries, Inc., a Christian counseling ministry in Rome. Keith had spent a lot of time with Nathan and Jane before going to Africa, and when he came back, we began to spend more time with them as a couple. We valued their friendship and insight so much that we asked them to do our premarital counseling. They now have a relational tool guide that we worked through called *Relationships*. It helped Keith and me learn powerful and practical ways to communicate with each other in our marriage. Because of their guidance, I began to learn how to express myself and identify areas of my heart that needed healing. I will be working on that until Jesus comes back, but first experiencing that small glimpse of freedom ignited a passion in me to help others. Jane and I soon started planning women's retreats to share the tools that were being taught in the counseling office. We are still leading women's retreats twenty years later.

Keith and I with Jane and Nathan in Canmore, Canada.

Nathan and Jane's relational tool guide.

Needless to say, Christy was right. I had met the man of my dreams, and we were married later that year on September 23, 2000. Keith had purchased a house on Little Texas Valley Road, and the backyard was a beautiful spot for a wedding. However, due to the weather that week, our plans to marry at our future home were dashed. It was a bittersweet day for me. I was really missing my mom, but

I was thankful to have the help of close friends, Chrystial Prater and Brenda Lyons. Chrystial was our pastor's wife and my wedding planner. I met Brenda at Coosa Middle School, where she was the receptionist. Her daughter died in a car accident at the age of sixteen, and my mom died when I was sixteen. We bonded through our tragedies.

The transition to married life was a lot more difficult than I expected. Since I had never been taught how to manage a household, and I had limited experience in a healthy, God-centered home, I felt that I did not know what I was doing as a wife and homemaker. I had a lot to learn. On top of that, Keith and I had a short courting period, and therefore, limited time to fully get to know each other. I did not realize how different we were. Keith was black and white, while I lived in "gray" land. He needed order and appreciated spreadsheets, while just the thought of that overwhelmed me. I wanted to keep things light-hearted and have fun. He expressed himself well and was very confident. I was always at a loss for words, and I shut down when things got hard. He was disciplined, and I was not. The differences I saw compounded my deep-rooted childhood feelings of being an inadequate failure. Needless to say, we had a lot of room for improvement.

In an attempt to strengthen our marriage, I bought the book *The Power of a Praying Wife* by Stormie Omartian. I was reminded of who my first love truly was, and I realized what I was doing was simply not working. I started praying and focusing on myself rather than Keith. When I did this, God was able to show me I was spending a lot of energy trying to fix things, which was exhausting.

The Lord was working on Keith's heart as well as mine. During the course of the next year, Keith had a dream. To this day, he feels that it was directly from the Lord. In this dream, Keith could hear a woman crying out in slow, pleading words, "Help me...". Keith listened to the woman's pleas as he began to wake. As he woke up, my breathing and the woman's cries became one. As I breathed in, the woman cried, "Heeelp...." and as I breathed out, she cried, "meeee." In the dream, I was so exhausted in my attempts to find peace in my relationship with Keith, that my very breaths were a cry for help. By God's grace, Keith finally "heard" me. He was broken. I had been crying for help, and I needed Keith's love and grace rather than his instruction and prodding. He was convicted. He tearfully asked for forgiveness.

I was numb. I was hurt and in disbelief. I was trying to grasp and receive what God was doing. I had been hoping and praying that He would do something, but I was in shock that this was really happening. I remember asking myself, "Is this really happening?" I couldn't believe it. I thought, "This is what I've been hoping for. Why isn't it going in?!" I was having a hard time receiving this new Keith. "What if it didn't stick?" I couldn't deal with another disappointment. I couldn't let my guard down. Even though in my brain I wanted to let my guard down, my heart wouldn't allow it.

Over the next days and weeks, Keith began to put energy toward being the husband God wanted him to be. We were determined to make this partnership work. Keith still describes this event as a milestone in our relationship. We knew that true, enduring change was a process that would take time, but we were committed to working it out during our marriage to one another

My Biggest Fear

One thing Keith and I both loved was hosting our life-group in our home on Little Texas Valley Road. Our singles group turned into a couples group, which grew into a big family. Many of these couples we still consider our family today. They helped us learn about the Lord, and His vision for marriage and family simply by doing life together.

Our Lifegroup, 20 years later, at CWR.

We were married two years when I found out I was expecting our first child, Caleb Miles. We were so excited as his due date got closer. Keith did not know we were having a boy, but I did. My friend, Lori, did my ultrasounds, and I talked her into telling me the gender. I did not tell Keith because I knew he wanted to be surprised!

In the midst of all this excitement and preparation for parenthood, I was still trying to convince my dad that he needed the Lord. I realized that it was not working. I stopped telling him about Jesus and simply started loving and serving him like Jesus. I finally began praying like I truly believed God would open his eyes because I knew that God was the only One Who could do this.

One day, out of the blue, my dad called to tell me that he had become a Christian. The pastor of one of his friends was visiting door-to-door that day. My dad rarely shared his emotions, but that pastor later told me that my dad opened up to him, and was broken. My dad wanted to proceed with getting baptized. The image of my giant dad standing beside the five-foot seven-inch pastor in the baptismal pool still stands out in my mind. By God's grace, my dad did not drown that day! God raised him out of that pool just like He raised him up spiritually. I remain thankful for faithful pastors and evangelists who serve in small rural churches all over the world.

I was so happy about my dad's decision to accept Christ, but something in me was also confused. I had been convinced that it had to be me who would lead him to the Lord. I felt that I was the only one who was truly present in his life, and as a result, I deserved to enjoy that moment with him. Needless to say, I was humbled by the fact that it was not me who led him to Christ. The Lord exposed my lack of faith, and I learned that it was not about me and my striving works. I just needed to do my part in being like Jesus in my interactions with my dad and then trust.

When Caleb was eight months old, we found out we were expecting our second child, Elijah Cole. Whether it was out of ignorance, or simply because of God's grace, I do not know, but we were so excited about having two little ones in the house. I loved having these two sweet boys in our growing family.

Around that time, my dad's health began to progressively decline. Dad had developed congestive heart failure and we thought it was time to move him closer to us. I had always feared his death, and I had played it out in my mind so many times. I feared the time was coming soon.

There was a lot going on in our lives. The responsibilities associated with taking care of two little boys, and an ailing father, began to take their toll. Keith and his business partners were very involved with growing a physical therapy practice that had expanded into four states and two separate lines of business. Keith was busy on the business front, which also required a fair amount of travel, and I was active on the home front.

Despite being in and out of the hospital that year, we had some sweet times. Special occasions brought him so much joy; he always wanted to give the perfect gift. That Christmas was tough. I had to call an ambulance on Christmas Eve because he was having a hard time breathing. When the ambulance got there, they put him on a ventilator. It was hard for me to see my dad like that, especially at Christmas. Thankfully, he was soon healthy enough to come home.

Keith was always supportive of me helping my dad, and it was he who suggested it was time for my dad to move in with us. Dad had to have dialysis, and his nurses who cared for him during his weekly visits became his best friends. I will never forget his doctor, Dr. Ware, and all the staff. Their invaluable kindness helped me get through each day.

This was one of the nurses where my dad had his dialysis treatments.

That following summer, Dad was admitted into the hospital yet again. He was admitted directly into the ICU, and we all knew that this time he would not make it out. I barely left his side. I will be forever grateful for all of the friends who helped us during those long, grueling days. He slept a lot over those two weeks, but we had rich, heartfelt conversations when he was awake. I think he was both scared and ready to go. I told him that Mom would be waiting for him and that I would be okay. He apologized profusely for being a burden. I responded by reminding him of what a great dad he was, especially when I was little. I told him that it was my privilege to now return the love to him. I was happy to be his caretaker.

Nathan, Jane, and Keith were there with me when Dad's passing became imminent. We noticed his breaths had become very slow and shallow. At the same time, his oxygen levels and heart rate began to decline. We called the nurse in as his breathing seemed to stop. The moment I had feared most of my life had arrived. We stepped out as they were checking on him, and I could only hold my breath as we held hands and prayed. I looked at the nurse through the window, and she nodded that my sweet, teddy-bear daddy was, indeed, gone. I remember taking a deep breath as I slowly looked up.

Somehow, I was okay.

As a matter of fact, I had peace. My heart was broken, but... ... I was also relieved. My heart flooded with emotions. I then became angry with myself for allowing Satan to rob me of peace and joy through the years. The thing that I feared the most, my dad's death, ended up bringing such reassurance of God's grace.

I still miss my sweet daddy, but I am reassured that he is now walking with Jesus. Perfectly.

Ironically, the deaths in my life ultimately ended up

saving my life spiritually. It was through these tragedies that I searched and found Christ. I ran to Him and wanted to know Him on a deeper level. He became my foundation. God's providence was evident throughout the ups and downs of my life. He provided me with the support I needed at every turn. The people that He placed in my life to intervene and encourage me were a gift from His hand. Often these gifts are how God's grace shows up during trying times. At this point in my life, I have watched God use His people to speak life into others when they need it most.

2.

Facing My Fear

The next year, Caleb began preschool at Unity Christian School (UCS) in Rome. I was also expecting our third child, a girl, Sydney Elise. When she arrived, the boys were uncertain about her at first, but they soon adjusted to life with a little sister. It did not take long for me to catch the boys sneaking into her crib to play with her. Although we did not know it at the time, Sydney would be the final addition to our family.

The boys sneaking into Sydney's room to play.

When Sydney was a year old, I started having health problems. I was not sure what it was, but I was having significant abdominal pain. I went to the doctor about the issues, but they did not realize how serious it was because I tended to downplay the discomfort. One day at home, the pain caught up with me, and I almost passed out in the hallway. I immediately went to the doctor, and they found that a cyst had ruptured on my right ovary. I was sent home and told to rest until they could schedule surgery.

The pain was very intense for the next few days, and the doctors finally decided to do exploratory surgery. During surgery, it became apparent that the removal of my right ovary was the best option. The rupture had caused significant blood loss, which is what had caused me to have the episode in the hallway. I'd already had three C-sections before, so that surgery marked my fourth abdominal surgery in five years.

The timing was awful because this happened to be the week of my sweet friend Hope Hite's high school graduation, and I was supposed to be hosting her graduation party. I was not able to attend the graduation, but a couple of my friends helped me carry out the plans for the party afterward. I met Hope when she was a teenager at The Church at Northside. Due to the difficulties of Hope's childhood and adolescence, she was living with her grandfather.

Hope's love for the Lord was inspiring. She helped me a lot with the kids, and she quickly became a part of our family. Although Hope was presented with so many potential barriers to success, she graduated valedictorian of her high school class. I was so proud of her. (Even now, I am thankful to have her help in editing my story.) After college, Hope married another friend of ours, Blake Frazier. We are partners with them in our car wash business in Louisville, Kentucky. They have a precious little girl named Frances and in June of 2020 birthed their second child, a sweet little boy, Ezra, into their family.

Hope and Blake's wedding at CWR.

I was so sure that removing my ovary was going to be the solution to my long road of abdominal pain. However, after surgery, the pain remained. Further studies were inconclusive, but it was likely that I had similar issues with the other ovary. We were faced with a decision. If we chose to remove the second ovary, it would send me into menopause at thirty-four years old. The thought of going from normal hormone production to none was scary. The physicians recommended the removal of my uterus as an alternate solution. I had my fifth abdominal surgery a few months later to remove my uterus. The doctors said that my left ovary looked good, so they left it to prevent early menopause.

A few months went by, and I remained in the same state of discomfort and discouragement. Neither the doctors nor I knew what was going on. Still, they said that this could happen, considering my history of multiple abdominal surgeries. When things did not improve, they finally suggested taking out my left ovary. I was just ready to feel normal again, so I agreed. This full hysterectomy ended up knocking the wind out of my sails! I felt worse, but the doctors reassured me that it would just take time to recover. I began experimenting with different hormones, but my body did not respond well. My lack of energy was the most challenging part of this entire ordeal. I had a hard time getting off the prescription pain medication because that was the only thing that would help me get through each day. However, I had faith that God was going to pull me out.

Although I was struggling, I continued hosting women's Bible studies in our home. One of these studies worked through a book entitled *Boundaries* by Dr. Henry Cloud and Dr. John Townsend. God used this book to change my life. It gave me permission to set limits and prioritize the demands of life. I needed to shrink my world and focus on my health and immediate family. One of my favorite parts of the book talks about the need for me to give myself permission to set healthy boundaries. I was hearing and learning that both parties need to be responsible for their own feelings of disappointment, hurt, anger, etc. I was used to trying to carry both mine *and* the other person's emotions. Now, I wanted to learn how to be responsible for my own emotions and carry them to Jesus. I could still care about the other person but not have to be responsible for them.

A summary of the book, *Boundaries,* puts it this way:

"Having clear boundaries is essential to a healthy, balanced lifestyle. A boundary is a personal property line that marks those things for which we are responsible. Boundaries impact all areas of our lives: Physical boundaries help us determine who may touch us and under what circumstances -- Mental boundaries give us the freedom to have our own thoughts and opinions -- Emotional boundaries help us to deal with our own emotions and disengage from the harmful, manipulative emotions of others -- Spiritual boundaries help us to distinguish God's will from our own and give us renewed awe for our Creator."

I had to analyze my relationships and listen as the Lord guided me in defining and establishing boundaries in my life. I experienced some difficulty in setting boundaries as a believer because I tend to feel selfish when making a decision based on what I need. Drawing these boundaries can be painful and create conflict. I lost a friendship during this transition of boundary-setting. Because of that loss, the Lord has taught me it is possible to hold both grief and a sense of peace at the same time. As our group finished the study, I began to see how listening to God's instruction in regards to boundaries was always the best choice for my heart.

The Choice

Life continued, but as I tried to manage my menopause symptoms, they did not get any better. I could not shake it. I did not feel like myself. I felt alone in my pain. This was one of those times I really missed my mom. Everyone, including me, wanted the energetic and happy version of Marsha back. Although I could usually perform my way out of my insecurities, I simply did not have the energy to keep up that charade. The "fake-it-'til-you-make-it" strategy I had been using was destroying me. I was shrinking and losing my sense of self-worth. I was hoping my medical team would find something they could treat. Test after test came and went. Normal results flowed in, bringing with them depression that became harder and harder to hide. My despair overflowed into our marriage.

Keith's work responsibilities grew as he and his partners continued to build the physical therapy business. This brought about new decisions they needed to make regarding the future of the company. These were stressful times for him. My health and the new stages in our kids' lives further complicated our family. Keith would admit now that he expected more from me than I could give. Once again, I needed his help, but he expected me to pull myself up by the bootstraps and shake myself out of it. We had a family to run, and he was too busy to pull me along. He admits to this mentality now, and, thank God, we both learned from these years of our lives together. But, it was a very lonely time for me. I found myself caught in a wave of shutting down, resolving to fix it, and pulling myself together. Over and over…

I began to think about how my prescription pain pills had helped me get through the day earlier in this journey. Then I heard the enemy's whispers of justification. I was reluctant at first, but then I began to listen. I was desperate. I convinced myself I would just take them until I found answers. The pain was no longer physical. Now the pain was mental, emotional…and unbearable. Taking care of the house and kids was the most important thing to me, and I could not do it. I was willing to do ANYTHING in order to bring peace to our home. To do this, I began to take a couple of pills each day. I felt like Paul did in Romans 7:19 (NIV), "For I do not do the good I want, but the evil I do not want is what I keep on doing."

Since I did not feel like God was helping me, I felt I had to take matters into my own hands. I created my own version of reality, which is a skill I am sure I developed at an early age. I lost sight of the truth, leaving myself to merely survive without listening to the voice of the Lord. I did not want to continue taking the pills, but I was tired of struggling. I would confess and cry out to God in hopes that the "next thing" would be the answer to my problems.

I got mad at God, and I hated myself. I tried to find ways to stay busy and distracted. I loved serving and helping others, and that made me feel a little better about myself. I justified my sinful behavior by feeling like I was the victim. I was just sitting in my sin, waiting for God to fix me. I now realize that repentance and obedience were necessary for His Spirit to move so He could meet my needs and bring healing to my spirit, soul, mind, and body. Even through this dark time, I prayed that God would use me in spite of me. Somehow, I held on to the tiny glimmer of faith I once had as I attempted to work hard at creating my own peace and joy. I now know that that is impossible. Just as only the Lord could open my daddy's heart to salvation, only He could be my true Source of peace and joy.

I wanted to tell Keith about using the pills but I felt sick when I thought about telling. I already felt like I was a disappointment to him because of my emotional struggles, so I could not bear the thought of him finding out about my secret. Life was simply too full. We were going through a lot of transitions, and it felt like the right time to deal with this problem never emerged.

In spite of my shortcomings, God was still at work in our lives and doing great things. God was opening doors for the creation of our camp ministry, which we envisioned to be a Christian retreat where we could create a nurturing environment for people to connect with God. Through a series of miraculous events, God dropped a little piece of heaven in our laps to share with others. It sits on top of the Cumberland Plateau in Tennessee, so we named it Cumberland Wilderness Retreat.

In the meantime, my brother, Barry, wanted to move closer to us. He and his wife, Deanna, moved from Pennsylvania and now live in Tennessee near our retreat. We are very proud of his son, Nate. He is a Staff Sergeant in the United States Army. He married his high school sweetheart, Alycia, and now they have a beautiful little boy named after my dad, Dawson William.

Barry, Deanna, Alycia, Nate, and Dawson.

Nate, Alycia, and Dawson.

We were selling our share in the physical therapy business, Advance Rehab, after Keith had been a partner with them for almost twenty years. We were trying to figure out what was next for us, which made for a stressful and scary time. We were working through the question of, "How do we live abundantly on this side of heaven?" Our hearts were open to anything the Lord would ask us to do, and we were willing to give everything up to follow Him. (And...I was hoping that maybe this next step would provide the peaceful environment I felt I needed to share my secret with Keith.)

Both Keith and I were deeply involved at Unity Christian School. I was teaching there part-time, and Keith was on the Board of Directors. He later became the temporary Headmaster. Unity Christian School is still very dear to our hearts, and we have always had a strong desire for it to be a successful place for educating children. They taught our kids how to develop a Biblical worldview, and because of the close connections that develop in a small community like that, the staff and kids at the school were like family to us. One particular student, Abigail Sorrow, had a significant impact on me. She has a contagious love for the Lord and has become a great writer in college. In fact, as I work on this memoir, Abigail is in the process of publishing her first book entitled, *Full*. Abigail was a vital part of helping me find the words to write my story.

Our three little ones in 2012, and our growing children in 2019.

Dandelion

One thing I have always admired about Keith is his honesty and willingness to stand firm in what he believes. It was this strength that initially drew me to him, and it was a quality I hoped to see develop in myself as well. As for me, my identity was too wrapped up in others and what they thought of me. I had so many strongholds and weaknesses that I had lost sight of Biblical truth. I realized I was running and trying to hide from the truth because it was too hard to face. I was still justifying my sin, and the truth was becoming more and more shrouded by my lie. Looking back over this hard time in my personal life, an analogy was taking shape in my mind. It involved the simple image of a dandelion. The French word for dandelion means "tooth of the lion." When the initial yellow flower first sprouts, it appears beautiful and strong. It eventually goes to seed and becomes weak and fragile. It is at this stage of the plant's life cycle that we see the familiar white powdery seeds that can be scattered with a gentle breath. My faith was so weak that I was allowing the dissatisfaction of Keith and others in my life to blow me away like the seeds of the dandelion. My world appeared strong and mighty to the outside but my sins would soon go to seed.

Alison Giddens gave my kids a book for Christmas that year called *Sidney & Norman: A Tale of Two Pigs* by Phil Vischer. She said that she thought of me when she read about Sidney. She knew most of my struggles and how hard I am on myself. I read the book and was just excited to relate to something, even a pig. In the story, Norman had it "all together," so he was proud and looked down on those that were not like him, and Sidney struggled and things didn't come quite as easily for him. Sidney felt broken. One day they both got a letter from God to come to visit. Norman was excited because he just knew that God would express how proud He is of him. Sidney was nervous and knew God would see right through him and say what a disappointment he is. He knew he couldn't fool God; He could see all his messes and mistakes. On the contrary, God told Norman that He loved him but that he was prideful and selfish. God told Sidney, "I love you"... And a second time, "I love you"... Then a third time, "I love you." Then God said, "That is all I wanted to tell you." Sidney was confused. Maybe he did fool God. He looked over at his reflection and noticed his tie was off-kilter, and his hair was rumpled so he couldn't have fooled anyone. He pondered the thought that "maybe God did indeed love me," messes and all. The truth that God loved him was sinking in...he started to stand a little taller and was glowing with a smile.

This may be a children's story, but God used it to remind me of His unconditional love. By no means is this an excuse for me to be messy or unorganized. I just have to work harder at the things that are strengths for the Normans out there. I longed for Keith to love and accept me, but in fact, that would not have been enough. Even if he had told me all I wanted to hear, I would still have a void that only the Lord can fill. It's amazing to watch how God uses our spouse's gifts and personalities to mold us into His likeness (if we let Him). This process can be very painful. I took my eyes off Jesus, my guard was down, and Satan's arrows found ways into my heart and mind. I was confused and slowly losing control.

At this point, Keith had finished his responsibilities with Advance Rehab, and we were free to go where the Lord was leading us. During this time of seeking the Lord's will for our family, Keith and I both felt led to move to Louisville, Kentucky. Keith was going to attend Southern Baptist Theological Seminary. He had already taken a couple of online classes, and the information was both challenging and practical. However, online education lacked the richness of human interaction and mental stimulation the classroom provides. After a brief visit to the campus, and continued prayer, we felt the liberty to dive headfirst into the seminary lifestyle. We wanted to be obedient and live the life God had for us. In my mind, the move was also an opportunity for me to get a new start. I was hopeful that in this new world I would find the strength I needed to slay my dragons.

Keith's parents, Earnest and Suellen, had recently made a move to Rome from Jonesboro, Georgia, to spend more time with the kids and us. However, during this transition, Keith's dad died from a sudden heart attack. After his passing, Suellen, who we call Nana, made the decision to move to Louisville with us. The six of us picked up and headed north, and we found a home with a fantastic basement apartment for Nana.

Our home in Louisville.

This move was a lot harder than I anticipated. I was totally out of my little comfort bubble. I felt lost and isolated. I was not with my kids at their school and I felt like I was losing them. They were becoming teenagers before my very eyes...more loss of identity. I was questioning my purpose. I was able to spend time with a couple of my best friends from Rome from time to time. Stephanie Reeder and Alison Giddens would meet me halfway and we would have lunch together or go shopping. These times blessed me and gave me something to look forward to. I loved having a little piece of Rome come visit.

Stephanie and Alison meeting me in Franklin.

After being in Louisville a few months, I was excited to find a hormone specialist who seemed like she really understood my story. Her unique perspective and personal experiences revived a fading hope in me that I could soon feel like myself again. I had previously tried several methods of hormone replacement therapy, and I did not respond well to any of them. Some of the treatments did nothing, and some made me overly sensitive and emotional/irritable. I was currently receiving hormone pellets that were inserted in my hip every three months. Because these were helping me feel a little more like myself, we continued this treatment.

Soon, however, my weaknesses surfaced, and it felt like salt being poured on an open wound. I love Nana dearly, and we are very close, but her strengths are my weaknesses. The enemy was using this to remind me of all the qualities I lacked. She enjoyed cooking, cleaning, and managing finances, and I did not have those strengths. I was jealous that she and Keith were able to talk about past memories that they shared. I did not have anyone who I could do the same with. The only immediate family member I still had left was my brother, Barry. But, he had his own journey to struggle through. Much of my life was lived apart from him. There was so much about my life I did not know or remember, but no one was around to ask. All of this made me miss my mom greatly. I didn't even have a single video of her. I considered trying to find those who received her organs when she died so that maybe I could find consolation in seeing a part of her still alive.

I was grasping for the wind and trying to find comfort. My new doctor suggested medications for depression and Attention Deficit Disorder (ADD). I took her advice, but I still felt like I was searching for an answer in what seemed like everything except for God. I was determined to fix myself by myself, so I bought a lot of books on how to do life better. Our family was home together a lot, which was hard at times. Not only was I adjusting to a new place, but I was also adjusting to Keith being home much more than usual. Nana was living with us, all of which accelerated the threat of exposing my internal struggle. I was running out of options for places to hide. I thought that maybe if I just tried harder things would get better. Meanwhile, it was becoming difficult to get the pain pills I'd been relying on to get through the day... for four years. This move to Louisville I had been hoping would be God's way of rescuing me out of my sin had turned into a tangled mess.

I had driven myself into a rut and was at a loss as to how I was going to get out of it. I had gotten so tired of trying to hide my struggles that I stopped covering up my destructive behaviors. It was obvious I was struggling. I started drinking alcohol to help ease the transition of trying to get off the pills. The sin and brokenness I was carrying was exhausting, but I still did not have the strength to tell anyone. I continued to ask God to deliver me. Sometimes, He answers in ways that are unexpected and painful.

Late one night in July of 2016, while we were at Cumberland Wilderness Retreat, Keith was headed outside and asked to use my phone as a flashlight. While he had it, he began reading several text messages I had wrriten. He discovered I had been buying prescription pain pills. When he confronted me about it, my world came crumbling down. Fear overwhelmed me. I could not breathe. I thought this would be a good time for God to take me. This moment is what I had dreaded. I feared we, Keith and I, would not recover. Exposure. I thought I had gone through my worst days of dealing with tragedies throughout my life, but this was truly the worst day because I had done this to myself and to my family. I realized I could not hide anymore. The exposure made me feel unsafe and vulnerable. My mom was the only person in my life who I had truly let into my soul, and I was terrified to let anyone else in, including Keith. I thought even he could not love me unconditionally as my mom did. This was the worst night of my life, but it was the beginning of my journey to freedom.

Going home that weekend from CWR was hard. I had no idea where my family and I were going to go from there. The hurt, confusion, anger, brokenness, and fear were more than Keith and I could bear. I had lost sight of Who and What was my real Source of hope. I had gotten caught up in a "crisis survival mode" way of living. Because of the many losses I had endured during my childhood, and the perpetual sickness in my adult life, I had begun to doubt the goodness of the Lord. I allowed the pain and discomfort I felt to become a destructive seedbed. I had also created a distorted view of the world and God. My hardened heart needed to be healed, and the only way was through breaking it. This brokenness, brought before the throne of God, was the beginning of allowing God to turn my mess into something beautiful. Keith was also broken and regretting not being there for me. I felt the Lord loving me through him, which brought so much comfort and healing.

We talked to Nathan and Jane who suggested a residential treatment facility in Chicago, Illinois called Timberline Knolls (TK). I was desperate, and willing to do anything to get better. We talked to the kids, and I went to this facility for three weeks. During that time, I saw the unhealthy coping mechanisms I had adopted. Through the years, I had felt the Lord touch my life, but He wanted my whole heart, not just the portions of it I was willing to give Him. TK was a place for being sequestered. Being sequestered meant that I had extended, uninterrupted time, free from distractions...to just "be." My work there was to slow down and pay attention to my heart, and to be curious as to why I had developed destructive patterns of coping. It provided the opportunity for the Lord to open my eyes and my heart.

As I looked back on my life while I was at TK, I wished I had had access to a place like that when I was sixteen. A place that could have helped me learn how to develop healthy habits. I truly believe it was God's grace that scooped me up before my life got any worse. I'm thankful Nana was there to help at home. I am also thankful for the support Keith received from his professor and friend, Jim Hamilton. He offered great advice and encouragement to both of us throughout this crisis.

In his seminary classes, Keith was learning about Biblical counseling. This concept was introduced to Keith through the writings of Christian psychologist and author, Paul David Tripp. The methods included some important distinctions that proved crucial to my ultimate healing. One of Tripp's books, *Instruments in the Redeemer's Hand*, had a significant impact on my transformation. It helped me understand more fully and practically what I already knew intellectually. Growing up in the "Bible Belt," I experienced a culture of knowing about Jesus and what the Bible was, but not truly understanding it deeply. This more profound understanding of the Gospel's power to heal and mend my brokenness melted my heart.

God also used Keith to bring healing to my heart. I was no longer fighting this battle alone. He was now by my side and I had nothing to hide. Keith's love touched me deeply. Though I feared he would not be able to love me the same as he did before, the fact was, he loved me more than ever. I was experiencing God's grace in the flesh and I wanted to embrace it. This was the beginning of me truly believing and accepting God's unconditional love.

As Tripp explained, "God's plan can be summed up in one sentence: people in need of change can help people in need of change. The Lord calls all of His children to participate in ministry all the time." Your ministry may be in your home taking care of your little ones, or it may be in the corporate office, making big decisions each day. In other words, God can use you wherever you are. I was determined to apply this teaching to my life by focusing on God's Word and learning who I really was in Him. One great benefit of being completely broken is that God can restore and mold you into His likeness. I was learning how to be the best wife and mom I could be and how to find contentment in that.

By God's grace I found a biblical counselor in Louisville named Lauren Bargas. She listened to my story and she cared about me while gently and constantly pushing me toward God's Word. We studied through a small, yet powerful book called *The Gospel Primer*. Because of my brokenness, my heart was tender and ready to receive God's Word in a new and fresh way. Lauren wanted us to go through the book very slowly, and repeatedly, so it would penetrate my heart. I did not truly believe that I was worthy of receiving God's grace.

A critical part of this process that Lauren and I were going through required my verbalization of what the Scriptures we studied meant to me. In verbalizing these truths, I realized I did not have a full understanding of what Jesus did for me. In my head I knew that Christ had died for my sins, but in my heart I could not receive any type of love and acceptance...from anyone (except my mom). And now, I had made all these bad choices. Could He really love me now? I was a failure and I had *chosen* to sin. I believed I actually *was* a failure.

Even so, I still wanted my light to shine. It seemed that receiving God's forgiveness was a key factor to my healing. I wanted to receive it but I just couldn't. I asked but did not feel that it was mine. Eventually, I realized that I needed to forgive myself as part of my healing. After I did this, I was able to receive God's forgiveness. I began to really absorb and understand that God's love for me does not depend on my choices. My status with God does not depend on me making great decisions in life. It does not depend on whether I get the kids to school on time, or if people are happy with me. God loves and accepts me. He values me...so much that He sent Jesus to die on the cross to rescue me from Sin. He loves me in spite of me.

Understanding all of this gave me the strength to be obedient (to make good choices) and trust Him with my life, which ultimately led to my healing. It was the right belief, which led to the right emotions, which led to the right behavior. My mom could not deliver me. My friends could not deliver me. Keith could not deliver me. It was so simple, yet so powerful. The correct understanding of the Gospel "saved" me. Ultimately, faith in Jesus saved me, but Lauren used the truth of the Scriptures to help me see Him more fully. Intentionally slowing down to ask God to help me make decisions, and trusting Him with the outcome, has made way for me to begin walking in peace and joy. (NOTE: This does not mean I am happy every day, but I do have peace.)

3.

Beautiful Mess

I went to Timberline Knolls (TK) one month after Keith found out about my secret. People have asked me what this facility was like because they usually envision a hospital-type setting, but this was more of a controlled dorm atmosphere. We had to follow a strict schedule, and we were not allowed to have phones or computers. They had twelve phones in a room we could use during certain times, and there was minimal privacy. I enjoyed the short walks to the cafeteria and to the counseling sessions. It was refreshing to meet with my counselor. She was a Christian and as she listened to me, she helped me begin to see significant parts of my story that I had minimized or been blind to. This was the beginning of my raw honesty with myself and others.

TK was mostly known for treating women with eating disorders, but they also helped women struggling with a variety of addictions, depression, and anxiety. All of us were just trying to figure out ways to cope with life. We had all experienced heartache, loss, chemical imbalances, pain, or abuse. We attended a variety of group sessions that focused on helping the group members be curious about their "why" that led them to their choices. These sessions also incorporated strategic ways to express what was going on in our hearts. We talked through our emotions and verbally dealt with our choices. We also used creative art therapy that helped when words were hard to express. This included movement, dance, yoga, and art.

The only thing I looked forward to doing while at TK was going to the art studio. It felt like home, and I did not want to leave. However, I was only able to go there two times a week. They limited the good things because even that could become another distraction or addiction. There was nowhere to hide. This new lifestyle of being exposed and vulnerable left me feeling really uncomfortable. I desperately wanted to find comfort in something. They let Keith bring me things to do during my free time, so I tried to crochet, paint, and color, but I soon grew tired of those. My last effort was beading. I had Keith bring me some jewelry beads and string during one of his visits.

During the transition to Louisville, I had started making bracelets as gifts for friends. I really enjoyed this type of craft. It gave me something to do during the long car rides from Georgia to Kentucky. Plus, I have always loved giving meaningful gifts. I was introduced to beading by Jane during an activity at one of our women's gatherings for Battlefield Ministries. She provided a variety of beads, stones, and string, and she asked us to pick out pieces that reminded us of the most memorable parts of our story. I did not know where to start, so I asked for the Lord's direction. I remember how that simple activity helped position my heart to better hear from the Lord. It was also a great visual reminder of what the Lord had done in my life.

After coming home from Timberline Knolls, Keith and I were determined to do life differently. We wanted to simplify our lives. We needed to shrink our world and focus on our family. We decided one way we could do this was to give up our iPhones. Yes, we went back to the old flip phone! The iPhone had become another source of distraction for me. I was always "on," and felt the need to respond to the outside world immediately. I carried an unnecessary urgency that created anxiety within my heart. I had forgotten how to just be, to allow feelings of boredom, and to simply sit with my own thoughts. Not having an iPhone was inconvenient, but I had a newfound peace. We went for a year without our iPhones. We have them now, but it does not consume me like it did before. I usually keep the sound off and respond when I am able.

I continued to pursue my new love for making jewelry. It was helping me clear my mind, slow down, and be present. I sometimes felt a nudge to make something specific for someone as a reminder of God's love. There is no greater feeling than being used by Him. I wanted to come up with a way to incorporate the Scriptures into what I was making, as a wearable reminder of the Truth, and this was when Beautiful Mess Gifts was born. I made a mess as I taught myself how to make jewelry, but I thought it was a beautiful mess. I know in the same way, God was turning my mess into something beautiful. I appreciate Keith letting me explore this new avenue of ministry in my life. Making jewelry did not feel like an important role, nor could it provide financially, but early in my recovery, it was the only way I could get quiet enough to hear God speak to me...And *that* was an important role.

In the fall of 2018, Jane and I led the women's retreat, "Come to the Garden." I took my crafts and jewelry for the ladies to "play with" during their free time. It was a fun time of fellowship and a great way to see everyone's personality shine through. Some got anxious as they were trying to figure out what they wanted to create, while others could not wait to dive in and start making something new. It was an excellent opportunity for them to learn more about themselves. As we walked through the activity, I asked questions about their favorite color, who they were making it for, important birthstones, favorite words, or Bible verses. I loved hearing their stories.

Several weeks before the retreat, I had started making a charm by gluing a Bible verse to leather and then cutting it out. I started to glue it onto a metal charm but began questioning myself, so I threw it back in the pile. At the retreat, my friend, Shani Sumner, noticed the charm and wanted to use it. I helped her make it into a bracelet, and we loved our creation! It is what I envisioned, but did not have the courage to do alone. She later sent me a picture of her wearing the bracelet, so I shared it on Facebook, and everyone loved it! I had about 100 people that wanted to order one! That certainly gave me a confidence boost to keep exploring my gift and sharing it with others.

This is my "Shani Bracelet."

1 Peter 5:10 (ESV) became my verse for Beautiful Mess Gifts. It says,

> *"And after you have suffered a little while, the God of all grace, who has called you to his eternal glory in Christ, will himself restore, confirm, strengthen, and establish you."*

Crafting at the women's retreat.

Another friend, Carrie Bishop, wanted me to do a local arts and craft festival with her. I hesitated because I was not sure if anyone would want to buy my jewelry. However, I thought it would be fun to hang out with her for the weekend, so I gave it a try. It was tough putting myself out there. I do not like feeling evaluated, and it is undoubtedly safer to stay hidden, but I did not want to miss out on what God had for me. The festival ended up being amazing! I loved meeting people and hearing their stories. Not to mention, I made some money while we were there! This experience gave me the confidence to go a step further, and I began to consider renting a booth in a local antique and art store. I called around town, but most of them did not have an open space. Finally, I called Nedra at Yellow Door Antique & Arts, and she said they had space. She walked me through the process, and I have had my jewelry booth set up there ever since.

God has used my business to transform my entire life. In the past, I was so concerned about others' opinions of me. That doesn't matter so much anymore. When I am working on different pieces, and I see that something beautiful comes out of the jumbled up mess of string and beads, it reminds me of my life. I want God to use me, all of the mess, and all of the beauty. If that means exposing my weaknesses, then so be it, and to God be the glory.

That is why I am writing my story. Kyle Idleman's book *Grace Is Greater* encouraged me to keep writing. Kyle's honesty and vulnerability reminded me that God's grace can transform the heart and rewrite a story that is worth sharing. Another truth from that book is that the Lord meets us where we are and graciously brings our sin into the light. Hiding our sin is terribly destructive. It provides Satan the power to keep us bound and blinded by it. God will use all of our story, the good and the bad, for His glory, as long as we let Him.

I got to know Kyle's wife, DesiRae, while our boys played lacrosse. Most people did not know what we were going through, but I felt like everyone could see my "scarlet letter," so it was hard to connect. I will forever be grateful for DesiRae's kindness and inclusivity. She was such a light while I was battling my darkness. It's true, you never know what people are going through, so offer grace, and be kind.

I have come to accept the life that God had planned out for me long ago: that plan included all of the losses I have experienced, but it also included my redemption. I am learning to hide His Word in my heart so that the things of this world will not look more attractive than Him. I am allowing Him to mold me as He desires. I am thankful He has opened my eyes so that His light can finally shine through me.

So, in the light of God's love, I choose to live, laugh, and love! (my mom's three favorite words)

4.

Truth-Family-Purpose

*I*n God's providence, our sovereign Lord had me (Keith) stumble across Marsha's secret at Cumberland Wilderness Retreat (CWR) in the middle of the night back in July of 2016. The revelation that Marsha had been fighting an addiction to pain medication was the door to a fortress she had built in an effort to protect herself from my insensitivity and pride. In other words, I had contributed to this crisis. I knew Marsha needed me. God had, in my opinion, supernaturally revealed that to me. But, I still pushed her instead of loving her. I knew that the moment that I uncovered the text conversation between Marsha and the provider of the medication. Marsha's problem was a Thompson Family problem.

CWR exists to strengthen families. The mission of

CWR is to reveal truth, empower the family, and discover purpose for the glory of God. Our gracious God built CWR through a series of miracles, and then, that night in July of 2016, led Marsha and me to the top of that mountain to provide our own life-saving Light. While I was navigating the tortuous journey of CWR's formation, God was building the means by which He would save our family. At the time, I had no idea. I simply knew, at the core of my being, that the God of the Bible was the answer to every person's problem. We longed to introduce people, in the most effective manner, to the One who promises rest and peace to a very broken world.

Marsha and I have always loved the outdoors. Our exposure to the work of Battlefield Ministries and Winshape Wilderness (now Winshape Teams) through their experiential approach to ministry had helped us value the unique advantages of slowing down and sequestering. We all know that our world offers many distractions. We also have experienced the life-giving clarity of those times when we were able to put away the distractions and narrow the focus to the one thing that seemed to be just what the doctor ordered. We were convinced that the disruption of a person's typical schedule and the displacement of their usual surroundings is fertile soil to discover a new, or be reminded of an old, message about life.

In fact, from the earliest days of our marriage, we had been thinking through how to transport, but still provide, the fellowship and Bible-based discussions that regularly took place in our living room in town. We wanted the setting to be free from the distractions of everyday life and be the door that would take believers deeper into the transforming doctrines of the Christian faith. The ideal experience would allow participants to spend extended time in a sequestered setting, to ponder the foundations of our faith, and apply them to their family and vocation. We had purchased a piece of property in north Floyd County on Everett Springs Road. The Everett Springs property had all the necessary building blocks for a unique retreat idea that had grown in our minds. The property had a creek and the topography required to build a 20-acre lake that would be situated parallel to and just below a 2500' long airstrip. Every camp needs a place to play in the water. The airstrip would serve as easy access for those who wish to arrive by small plane as well as serve as an athletic field. Of course, none of this was on the property yet, but the possibilities were there. As we prayed through the development of this piece of property it just never seemed to come together. I have experienced God's miraculous work in different phases of my life. I have grown to know that He has a distinct way of moving in my life and His timing is perfect.

In the winter of 2012, I was in a board meeting with my business partners and received an email from Jason Free. Jason is a realtor who was very familiar with our dreams of developing a camp ministry. I could not believe what I was reading. He had found an enormous piece of property that he thought we would be interested in looking at. The property was presented for sale in three tracts of 1200 acres each. Any one of those tracts was way more than we needed, or could afford, but this particular property had to be bought together. All 3600 acres had to be purchased as one piece. This property was simply not what we were looking for. But, something crazy grabbed my attention and almost brought tears to my eyes. The property had a 73-acre lake with a 4,500' long grass airstrip right beside the lake. I could not believe it. As soon as I saw the property, the Lord began to stir in me a possible journey to acquiring the property to build a ministry where we could introduce people to Him and the life-changing message of the Gospel.

Unlike the Everett Springs property, the doors began to fly open. One door would swing open, and another one would shut. The journey from a dream property that popped up in my email during a business meeting, to God laying the property in our lap to use for ministry, is filled with too many miracles to recount here. We began a project to raise money using various strategies. God brought so many people to the table to help us bring the camp to life. Business associates, friends, and complete strangers all played a part in putting the project together. Nate and Jeanie King were crucial at the beginning of the project. I had the dream and the general framework for how I thought the Lord would bring the project to fruition. If the dream the Lord gave me was the foundation and the structure, the Kings helped provide the drywall, paint, and flooring.

One particular relationship proved critical. Matt Campbell and I had known one another for a long time and had even been co-owners of a small airplane together. Although we had discussed the project in its early phases, I had not heard from Matt for quite a while. One day, he called to tell me that there was an outside chance that a business associate of his might be interested in our project. Matt and I headed down to Atlanta and met with his contact. After sharing our story and vision, we planned to meet on the property and discuss the project. By God's sovereign hand, and after one month of conversations, Matt's contact funded two-thirds of the project. It was a miracle. I simply did not have the resources or contacts to fund the project. Yet, I never really doubted that God would make it happen. We invested quite a bit of our own money creating the structure for the deal. That money would have been lost if God had not come through. But He did. He always had.

So, we waited and found ourselves at the head of a

501(c)3 organization named Cumberland Wilderness Retreat.

It is difficult to understand our family's story without CWR. God has woven CWR into the framework of our family life. Since 2013, spring, summer, and fall are littered with trips to camp to enjoy friends and family, prepare for upcoming camps, perform maintenance and repair work, and do our best to lift up the glorious Name of Jesus to anyone who will listen. Our retreats usually last at least two days. If we had to nail down a distinctive for CWR, it is a desire to link all practical ministry, which includes marriage, parenting, relationship skill-building, and overcoming addiction, with solid Biblical truth. We hope to help Christians think through the "why's" of our worldview. This is a challenging task to do one 35-minute sermon at a time. On the mountain, we have time to think through Biblical truth, discuss it, let it simmer while we are enjoying the property, and then come back together to build on it while it is still fresh on our minds.

One last thing about CWR... The Bible tells the story of King Solomon receiving a visit from the Queen of Sheba. She had heard of his greatness and the greatness of his God. She came down to see it for herself. Once it was all said and done, she remarked, "Your wisdom and prosperity surpass the report that I heard. Happy are your men! Happy are your servants, who continually stand before you and hear your wisdom!" (2 Chronicles 9:7, NIV). Jerusalem and the temple of Solomon's God are literally on a hill. In His Sermon on the Mount, Jesus said, "You are the light of the world. A city set on a hill cannot be hidden" (Matthew 5:14, NIV). The temple, as people know it, is no longer God's dwelling place. The people of God are the new temple. He dwells in, and with, and through us. There is something miraculous that happens when God's people gather together, focus on Him, then interact with one another in a way that glorifies Him. God's wisdom, manifested in His people, who are the new temple of God, has the power to change lives and declare His glory to people like the Queen of Sheba, who have never experienced Him. God's truth, demonstrated through healthy families and lived out every day in vocations all over the community, is transformative. It is at the heart of the Gospel.

And then, there is that trip to CWR in July 2016, when I grabbed Marsha's phone for a source of light, and actually was provided with a different, more necessary life-light. I am thankful for the Lord's providence, and for His kind, gentle, wondrous truth. Our family needed to be rescued. I love the fact that God began that process on that mountain. It is a special place, and the stories that have been told there and have been begun there are a blessing that we do not deserve but for which we are beyond thankful. We extend a welcome to you, wherever you are, to come visit us. The property is the Lord's. One thing is certain: God is in control of His world. If you are reading these words, it is not an accident. Consider this a personal invitation from a personal and gracious God to come hear from Him at CWR. You can even come by yourself! Either way, just come and see what He may have for you there. You never know, you may find a miracle of your own, much like we did.

Our first family camp at CWR 2014.

A beautiful waterfall at CWR.

An aerial view of CWR.

Fun for all ages at CWR!

Just a boy and his dog.

Staying on the ground simply isn't as much fun...

5.

A Promise Fulfilled

Keith has three older sisters, Kathy, Karen, and Robin. Robin's husband Andy played an important role on the moutain. Keith and Andy spent a lot of time together after we started CWR. Andy helped us develop the property. He could fix anything, but he especially enjoyed working on and operating the tractor. He loved every minute of it. It was fun watching Robin and Andy create their safe haven on top of that mountain, and the process also seemed to bring them closer together as a couple. God used CWR to transform Andy, but that process really started years ago. Robin was not happy in the early years of their marriage, but she was committed to making it work. She prayed until the Lord turned Andy's life around. I asked her to share her story of redemption.

Robin and Andy

Robin's Story

I love to tell my story. It's a story I could tell over and over again to anyone willing to listen. I was serving in Sunday School one day, and a lady asked me about my story. So, I took a deep breath, and in my passionate southern accent, that causes me to talk ninety-miles-a-minute, I shared my story. I did not stop talking for more than thirty minutes! That poor lady who asked, she will probably never serve with me again!!

I was your typical southern girl. I was born and raised in church. Sunday mornings, Sunday nights, Wednesday nights, Mission Friends, Sunbeams, Girls in Action… should I say more? My life was the church. Mom and Dad sang in the choir, while their very young children sat in the front pew. By all appearances, we were a very religious family. Andy's background was somewhat the same.

From a very young age I was taught the Word. I knew the Bible stories, and most importantly, I knew the greatest story of all—the story of how Jesus came and died for me so that I could live. So as a good Baptist girl would do, I walked the aisle of the church, knelt at the altar, and prayed the sinner's prayer, asking Jesus into my heart. My Christian "checklist" was complete, and that meant I was saved, right? Andy's background was somewhat the same.

Christianity became an emotion for me. I would feel bad about what I did, and then instantly go to the altar, or get on my knees, confess my sin, receive God's forgiveness, and make promises of never doing that particular thing again. The process of repentance always made me "feel" better. However, I was only changed in that moment. I believed that if you sinned, God would forgive you. But I never realized there was more. I believe most Christians walk this way. We bend our knees in the midst of the guilt from our sin, and feel the power of His forgiveness. We never realize that we can arise from that place, be freed from the power of sin, and walk into a new life.

As I grew older, I continued to try to do the right thing. I tried to be a good girl and make the right choices instead of living out of the wrong choices that I made or that were done to me. However, I never had the power to say "no" to the lies in my heart that said, "this time will be different." Those choices always led me down a path of destruction, creating unhealthy patterns. I eventually stopped trying to be "good" and became a woman fully engulfed in a life of sin.

My first job was a bank teller. One day, a young man walked up to my window, and my life was changed forever. One thing led to another, and we started dating. This young man's name was Andy Dixon, and he swept me off my feet. He was my knight in shining armor. I had never felt so loved by anyone as I did by him. I knew that he was what my heart had been longing for. We were married on September 23, 1983. Soon after our wedding, Andy's armor fell off.

In the first five years of our marriage we had what some would call the picture-perfect life. We had our first home, two children, and money in the bank. However, on the inside, things between Andy and I were far from good. Time has a way of revealing the reality of things, and over time, our heart's grew cold toward one another. Our marriage was a living hell. Neither marriage, family, money, nor things could fill the empty void in our hearts. We started looking for love in all the wrong places.

God began to draw me to His side through a series of events in my life. I quit my job at the bank to stay home with the boys, and I started taking them to church. I had not been to church since Andy and I got married, and it felt good to be back. This was not the case for Andy. He did not like the ways of the church, and he never went with me. His heart had grown so cold over the years, especially toward God. He was very jealous of my relationship with the church, with God, and with anything that took me away from him. You see, I was Andy Dixon's wife, and no one, not even God, was going to have me.

I met an incredible lady at church named Shirley. She became a mentor to me and a dear friend. One unforgettable day, she looked at me and asked me a question that would change my life forever. She said, "Robin has God ever shown you that you are a sinner in need of a Savior?" I replied with a simple "No." I did not understand what she was asking me, but she encouraged me to ask the Lord to show me. You see, Shirley saw me—she really saw me—and I trusted her with my story and my heart. She listened to my struggles, and she knew what I needed. I needed a revelation of Who Jesus was to me.

In my mind, I thought Andy was going to be my savior because he promised to love me and take care of me. He was a man who could literally do anything. He built our home and he fixed our cars. He was independent, and he was self-sufficient. However, his greatest strength was also his greatest weakness. He needed no one, not even God.

Over time, I began to consider Shirley's question more and more. I studied the Bible and what Jesus meant to my life. God opened my eyes, and I could see clearly. We have heard it, and we even sing it, in the famous hymn Amazing Grace—"T'was blind, but now I see." I could see myself in light of Who God was. I saw my sin, yet I saw His forgiveness. It is hard to put into words. In an instant, there was this exchange of my life for His.

Over the next year, I tried to be good for God. I tried so hard to love Andy, and be the Christian woman God would be proud of, but at every turn, I failed miserably. One night crawling out of bed so as not to wake Andy, I knelt before the Lord in great desperation. With all honesty, I told God I was done. Honesty is something that I could give God. Actually, it is all I could give Him. I was done with my marriage, and done with Andy. I had so much anger in my heart from my past, and it was all aimed at Andy and our life together. I cried out to God that night, and pleaded with Him asking, "Either you get rid of him [Andy], or save him." I thought that either way, I would get a new husband. God spoke to my heart, not in words that man could hear, but my heart heard them. My heart heard Him say, "It is done, Robin!! Now rise from this place, and love Andy with the love of God." That night God filled me with His love in a supernatural way. His life for my life. His love for my hate. I was starting to understand what it meant to allow His Life to live through me. Only God can open our eyes through revelations of His ways, and leave our hearts changed forever. That is exactly what happened to me. My heart was changed.

I would love to tell you that things changed immediately for me and Andy after that night, but they did not. The next few years were the hardest of my life. I began to learn how to take God at His Word, and stand on His promises. God told me that Andy would be saved, and that was the easy part. That was God's part. The hard part was to allow God's love to come in and transform my heart, so that I could love a man I hated. I had to walk in dry places with no emotional love to lean on. The only thing I had was God's Word. God wanted me, and He was calling me to choose Him. Sounds easy, right? I knew one thing was for sure: I loved God more than I hated Andy.

On Sunday nights, our church would gather for a time of prayer. We would share our prayer requests, and then kneel at the altar and pray. Andy was always on everyone's hearts. They knew our story, and stood with me in prayer. One night, I remember standing and asking for a very bold request. I asked my church to stop praying for Andy's salvation, and to start praying for me. Andy's salvation was done. God had promised that to me years before, but I knew that without God's help, I would not survive to see His promise fulfilled. Life was too hard.

God gave me Galatians 2:20 which says, "I have been crucified with Christ, and I no longer live, but Christ lives in me. The life I now live in the body, the flesh, I live by the faith of Christ, who loved me and gave Himself for me." This is the exchange that I experienced, and still experience, to this day. I no longer live my life, but Christ lives it through me. People see me, but I see Him. It is a beautiful exchange, but the hardest thing I have ever done.

Seven years passed after I cried out to God and received the promise for Andy's salvation. In the summer of 1997, during Vacation Bible School, my youngest son, Thomas, received Jesus as his Savior. He shared his decision with us, and wanted to make it public the following Sunday at church. This opened the door for Andy and I to talk about the Lord, and I remember him telling me that he wanted to make that same decision as Thomas did. Andy had started going to church with us, and God had started drawing him to His side. Through the love that God had given me for him, Andy was able to see the love of the Lord. I knew first hand what it meant when the Scriptures said, "there is no greater love than to lay down one's life for one's friends" (John 15:13).

I watched as the Lord brought Andy face to face with his life. I watched as he saw himself in light of Jesus' love for him. I saw him experience his own Gethsemane. That Sunday night, all three of the boys walked together down the church aisle, and yes, you betcha, I was there, too. Andrew, my oldest had already given his life to Christ, but wanted to make a new commitment. The four of us stood together, publicly, rejoicing in the goodness of God. Only my boys, myself, my family, and our church family truly knew what took place that day. We saw a miracle happen, and we will never be the same. Praise God!

During those seven years of waiting, I learned how to take God at His Word, no matter what I felt or saw. I used that power to fight the enemies of my heart that tried to kill, steal, and destroy the promise that God had given me for Andy. God healed our marriage during those seven years. The love that God had given me changed my life, which ended up changing Andy's. The love we receive from God changes us so that we can give it away to others.

As life continued, Andy struggled to find his place in church. He tried to be something for God that God had not created him to be. He was a worker, and he knew that he had a job to do somewhere. He tried teaching Sunday school, leading the youth group, running the sound system at church, and many other things. However, he never found the joy he knew that he was created for until he found his place at CWR. These are Andy's words that he wrote as a testimony.

"I've been called a workaholic many times. I say I have a project-oriented personality. I do my best thinking while steadily working. Thanks to a loving God, and a praying wife, I gave my life to the Lord in 1997. Many times over the years, I have asked my wife, "Why did God make me this way? Why do I never feel completely fulfilled? Why, why, why"... And then came Cumberland Wilderness. The first time I sat foot on the property, I knew the Lord had answers for me there. I get great joy seeing someone's jaw dropping expression when they see the place for the first time. Knowing that I was allowed to have a small part in them finding the Lord there, fills my heart. So thank You, Lord, Cumberland Wilderness, and Keith for allowing me to have a part, and to find and accept God's will in my life and my purpose in His Kingdom. I now know that all my whys have but one answer- "For His Glory."

Andy had a dream one night after he started working at CWR. In the dream, he was sitting on a horse at the top of the mountain, and as he sat on the horse, he looked down the mountain and saw people gathering there. He had worked for weeks preparing for their arrival, and everything was ready for them. He could see the looks on their faces as they climbed the mountain. Their joy brought him even greater joy. He knew his job was complete. He then rode off in fulfillment of his purpose.

Andy loved the mountain and had dreams of living there one day. He spent most of his time there. From early spring, to late fall, you would find him there cutting the grass, taking care of the lakes, the runway, and the orchard. His time there alone with the Lord spoke louder to him than any sermon ever could.

In 2017, Andy started getting sick. We noticed his speech was slurring. Through many doctor visits, he was finally diagnosed in March 2018 with amyotrophic lateral sclerosis, commonly known as ALS. Even then he continued his work on the mountain. Little did he know that November 2018 would be his last time on the mountain.

I have no words to describe the suffering that Andy went through. He lived only one year after his diagnosis, passing away on March 7, 2019. The night Andy passed away, I found myself once again in a desperate place, falling on my knees and asking God the very same thing I did in 1987. I never knew I would pray those words again 32 years later. This time my heart was different, and I prayed, "Lord please take him or save him." I desperately wanted him to live, but hours later God took Andy home to be with Him. As I write these words, Andy has been gone for only ten months. His presence, at times, still seems so real, and so close. Andy and I were very close, and our love for God, and each other, was so tangible. Our love was a reminder to both of us how much God loves us, and that is what marriages are supposed to be—a picture of God's love.

At Andy's gravesite, his marker reads, "A tangible fulfillment of God's love." Mine and Andy's life together was that very thing, a promise fulfilled.

The Silent Warrior

(Andy's Eulogy by Keith Thompson)

Andy spent sixty years here making an impact on so many. I couldn't get much of anything done on the property at CWR without him. Doing life with Andy compelled me to coin a new word: "Andified." So, to help expand y'all's vocabulary, here is a new word. Andified: (It's an adjective) – if something has been Andified, it has been made better. The word is usually used in reference to a process, a piece of equipment, or a landscape.

Andy was always working, but he was almost always working on something for someone else. He was quick to move to the back of the crowd, or to just leave the crowd behind. Andy's quiet personality could give the impression that he did not love people, but that would be a significant misrepresentation of who he was. He loved people in his own priceless way. He served them. Steadfast love manifested in dependable faithful service. That's Andy Dixon.

No, Andy was not a man of many words, but for me, what he did say mattered. When working through a project up on the mountain, he was always slow to make a recommendation. But, if asked, he would always throw in his two cents worth of wisdom. Whether you took the advice or chose another plan, he was simply faithful to do his part. That is the hard part. He did not have to get his way, or be right, he simply served.

In the spring of 2013, after we acquired the property on the mountain, I got a call from him. He had been up to see the place and to hear our vision of creating a Christian family ministry there. His visit to the property had a significant impact on him.

The Christian ministry world tends to elevate certain gifts and certain kinds of people. This is not always the case, but it is often the case. The ones with the dynamic personalities, the moving speakers, and the powerful voices. The "up-front folks" are sometimes venerated in a way that could induce the Andy's of the world to feel unable to contribute. Andy told me that day that he had recently struggled to find his place, his vocation, his calling, so to speak, in the work God was doing in the world. He longed to contribute, but just could not find his place. He began to weep, and told me that when he was on the mountain, he knew he had something to contribute. He wanted to know if I thought I might be able to find a spot for him in helping us take care of the place. Can you imagine Andy Dixon feeling incapable? It's absurd, really. Please hear me say that his struggle to find his place in ministry was not an indictment on any particular church where Andy may have attended. But, it is a picture of what the enemy has set out to do in all of us. The Apostle Paul reminded the church in Ephesus that "we do not wrestle against flesh and blood, but against the rulers, against the authorities, against the cosmic powers over this present darkness, against the spiritual forces of evil in the heavenly places." (Ephesians 6:12, NIV). Jesus Himself, referring to Satan as a thief, asserted that our enemy "comes to steal, kill, and destroy" (John 10:10).

We have all been created in God's image. He has placed his stamp on us, and in us. It is there, whether we acknowledge it or not. The Christian worldview asserts that we human beings live in two worlds: one ruled by God, and one ruled by Satan, the enemy. Satan cannot take away the gifts God has placed in us. They are meant for the good of Christ's Kingdom. But, the enemy can hijack those gifts, rendering them useless. Paul used the analogy of a soldier to describe a Christian. Among other things, the soldier is equipped with a sword, a helmet, and a shield. The most competent and magnificent warrior in any army, at any time, is ineffective if he believes he is in the wrong battle. The enemy does the most damage to a human being, not by killing him, but by convincing him that he is useless, unworthy, too damaged, or too far gone to fulfil his purpose and complete the mission.

In Romans, Paul reminds us that everyone has sinned, thus demonstrating our inability to live up to God's glory.

Sin is not a very fashionable word these days, so I will put it another way. We have all acted in a way that is inconsistent with our purpose. Only the Creator of a thing can decide its ultimate purpose. In many ways, we have all betrayed that purpose, and because we have betrayed that purpose, we have betrayed God. Human beings do not fare well when they betray God. We can shake our fists at Him, but at the end of the day, His forgiveness is our only hope. The God of the Bible is the God that is there, and the One that has chosen to reveal Himself to us in Creation and in Scripture. God stands before us, before you, even this afternoon, and offers forgiveness through faith and trust in Christ. The prophet Isaiah reminds all of us that our rebellion against God has created a barrier between us and the Lord. However, Christ is the great Reconciler.

The Apostle Peter, speaking of those who have placed their trust in Jesus, said in 1 Peter 1:3-7,

> *"Blessed be the God and Father of our Lord Jesus Christ! According to his great mercy, he has caused us to be born again to a living hope through the resurrection of Jesus Christ from the dead, to an inheritance that is imperishable, undefiled, and unfading, kept in heaven for you, who by God's power are being guarded through faith for a salvation ready to be revealed in the last time. In this you rejoice, though now for a little while, if necessary, you have been grieved by various trials, so that the tested genuineness of your faith—more precious than gold - that perishes though it is tested by fire—may be found to result in praise and glory and honor at the revelation of Jesus Christ".*

I know this is a bold claim, but I would suggest to you that without Christ, there is no hope. With Christ, our future hope is absolutely certain. The Apostle John wrote the last Biblical biography of Jesus' life. At the end of the book, he clearly states why he wrote it, saying, "Now Jesus did many other signs in the presence of the disciples, which are not written in this book; but these are written so that you may believe that Jesus is the Messiah, the Son of God, and that by believing, you may have life in his name" (John 20:30-31, NIV).

Andy's last six months were rough. His last forty-eight hours were rougher, but his circumstances were never hopeless. We left him Saturday to head back home to North Georgia, and on my way out, he mouthed, "Hey, it's going to be alright." I cannot explain the peace we all felt in those last hours, nor the peace we feel now. The Bible says that the peace of God surpasses all understanding, and we feel it in times like this (Philippians 4:7).

The book of James reminds us that we don't know what will happen tomorrow. James asks, "For what is your life? It is a vapor that appears for a little time and then vanishes away" (James 4:14). There is something that just feels wrong with the speed at which time passes. The older we get, the more amazed we are that time has passed so quickly. I used to spend my days working in hospitals as a physical therapist. When I had the opportunity to work with patients in their 90s or older, I would always ask them, "What words of wisdom do you have for a young man like me?" They almost always urged me to understand that life passes so quickly. Don't waste it.

Life is short, eternity is long, choose wisely.

If anyone had told me back in 1993, when I moved to Rome, Georgia, to begin my life as a physical therapist, that I would likely end the last half of my life doing ministry on a piece of property that God would drop in our lap, on top of a mountain with 3600 acres, beautiful 40 mile views, lakes, a grass airstrip, and that Andy Dixon would lead the way in managing the property for the glory of God, I would have told you that is impossible. Both about the property and about Andy. My faith was not as strong back then, but the Christian God is a miraculous God. He did not choose to heal Andy's ALS in 2019, but the miraculous life He gave Andy in 1997 was a far greater miracle. I'll read three verses from II Corinthians 4 and close:

> *"So, we do not lose heart, though our outer self is wasting away, our inner self is being renewed day by day. For this light and momentary affliction is preparing for us an eternal weight of glory beyond all comparison, as we look not to the things that are seen but to the things that are unseen. For the things that are seen are transient, but the things that are unseen are eternal" (v. 16-18).*

6.

Cultivating Peace

A Biblical Perspective with Lauren Bargas

*I*n the Fall of 2019, I was planning a women's retreat at CWR. This was my first retreat since 2016, and as I was praying for direction, I felt that "peace" was the topic the Lord wanted me to focus on. My perspective on peace had changed over the years. I used to think that peace automatically came with being a Christian, but now, I believed that it was a wonderful gift that the Lord wanted to give me. The word "cultivate" also kept coming to mind during my planning times. Cultivate means to prepare and use the land for crops or gardening. Our hearts are much like soil. They also need to be cultivated and prepared for what the Lord wants to plant in them. One way to ready our hearts is by being honest with Him and confessing our sins. Psalm 51:17 (NIV) says, "The sacrifices of God are a broken spirit; a broken and contrite heart, O God, you will not despise." Confession is the process that tills up the heart and gets us in a position to receive from Him. We also need to study His Word, which plants the seeds of life. The Psalmist wrote in Psalm 119:11 (NIV), "I have stored up your word in my heart, that I might not sin against you." Once you get to a place where you can store God's Word in your heart, the Lord will do the rest of the work.

The Holy Spirit supernaturally helps us grow, but we have to continue seeking Him. The weeds, which is our sin, always try to creep back in. The disciple Luke talks about two ways our hearts can receive seeds from God.

> *"The seed that fell among thorns stands for those who hear, but as they go on their way they are choked by life's worries, riches, and pleasures, and they do not mature. But, the seed on good soil stands for those with a noble and good heart, who hear the word, retain it, and by persevering produce a crop" (Luke 8:14-15).*

The desire of your heart should be to cultivate the good soil so that God's words can penetrate your soul.

I felt like the Lord was showing me that "Cultivating Peace" needed to be the theme of the retreat. I was able to get Lauren, my counselor from Louisville, to come and speak to us. She gave a wonderful message about developing a Biblical worldview and how we can use God's truth to guide our thoughts and actions. The following is my synopsis of what she spoke to us that day.

Lauren teaching at the women's retreat at CWR.

"It would seem everyone is searching for peace at one level or another. But what is it? It seems a bit elusive. Simply flipping through Netflix shows will tell you that. There are documentaries, comedies, and dramas, all with underlying messages about what the answer is to inner peace. Some say the answer is love, and that you just need to find the right spouse among the billions of choices you have. Maybe it is through a passionate religious experience, or perhaps it is through gaining control of your body by eating right and lifestyle changes. Maybe it is through eliminating toxic relationships, or finally discovering the nationality of your ancestors, and thus the history and makeup that defines you. Or, perhaps it is through a fulfilling career and ultimately achieving the title you want. It could be "letting it all go" in the name of travel and discovering other cultures.

But, under it all, the message is this: do what makes you happy and don't let anyone tell you differently. Perhaps it is a little more simple for you. Maybe you define peace in your own life as a lack of open and apparent conflict with people you love. It is perhaps merely attaining what you would consider a good life. But, herein lies the problem: It is a futile pursuit. The search always continues with chasing after something new that promises peace. Marriages and careers fail. Wealth leaves us only wanting more. Eliminating toxic relationships causes uncomfortable moments, gossip, and other relational tension. We fall back into no exercise and poor eating, and discovering who your ancestors are may be more disappointing than fulfilling. So, to keep some measure of peace in our lives, we do whatever we can to juggle all of life's complications and heartache. We strive to keep any semblance of peace by sweeping conflict under the rug, gossiping to make ourselves look and feel better, engaging in retail therapy, and defining "me time" as essential, even at the expense of those we love. Sometimes, we try to hold together the threads of what little peace we do have, intent that our happiness is so essential that it merits abandoning loved ones, using drugs, or other escape routes.

Have you noticed that at every turn in life, something is vying for your peace? Something is always attempting to nag at your mind or threaten your happiness. That comment she made. That thing he did. That text you saw on your daughter's phone. So, why aren't our cures for happiness working? What is missing? Why are we caught in endless cycles of pain and discouragement? Why are suicide and depression and anxiety becoming epidemics? Why is there so much hurt and loneliness? If the answer is to do what makes you happy, then why aren't we happier?

The real answer may surprise you. Jesus tells us the key is the heart. We know it is a vital organ, and metaphorically how we might express our love for someone. It is also the theme of Valentine's Day. But, the Bible actually talks quite a bit about the heart and defines it as essential to understanding people. In Ephesians 3:16, the Bible breaks a person down into two beings: the outer man and the inner man. The outer man is the physical body, or what you can see on the outside. The inner man is everything inside, including the spirit, soul, mind, emotions, and will. The heart of a person is shorthand for the whole inner man. The heart is the core of who you are and the control center for every person. It answers the question, "Why do people do what they do?" Consequently, your heart is at the center of any struggle for peace. It could be a struggle with spiritual peace between you and God, or relational peace between you and others. There could be a struggle for peace in your life between what you want and what your reality is. It is the root of and the reason for your actions. So, the heart is a pretty important piece to the puzzle of cultivating peace.

Think about what I just described in terms of a tree with a root and fruit. The root is the heart, and the fruit is the action. One of the reasons a tree is used to illustrate the concept of the heart is because of Luke 6:43-45 (ESV). It says, "For no good tree bears bad fruit, nor again does a bad tree bear good fruit, for each tree is known by its own fruit. For figs are not gathered from thornbushes, nor are grapes picked from a bramble bush. The good person out of the good treasure of his heart produces good, and the evil person out of his evil treasure produces evil, for out of the abundance of the heart his mouth speaks." We see here that a person's actions come directly from the heart. A good heart produces good words and actions, and an evil heart produces evil words and actions. A person's words are telling of what is going on in their heart. You can know a person's inner man by the fruit that they produce.

The problem is the heart, not the circumstances. When the heart is left unchecked, the actions will reflect that. A good example is a teabag. The heat from the water literally draws out the contents of the teabag or the contents of the heart. Oftentimes, we respond by blaming others for our actions. We may say things like, "He made me so angry," "I would not have responded that way had you not said that," "If I just had more sleep," "If I was able to explain myself," "If I just had this house, or more money," or...any of these excuses. These situations simply draw out what is already in your heart. Blaming others for your feelings can lead to a slippery slope of not taking responsibility for your own peace.

Now that we have looked at how the heart is our control center, there is one more component to the heart that you must know about. But, let me tell you, it is a trap that ensnares everyone. The trouble with the heart is that it is never neutral. It is always worshipping something, whether that be sin, an idol, or Christ himself. The heart's original intent and design is to worship God. Instead, because of sin, the heart has turned to itself to "worship and serve the creature rather than the Creator" (Romans 1:21-25, ESV).

There is always a battle taking place in our hearts--a fight to believe that God is good and is for us. It is a fight to love God with our whole heart, soul, mind, and strength, as we are commanded. What this means is that our hearts should be fighting to worship God every moment of every day. When we win this fight, there is true inner peace. The less we believe God is working for our good and our peace, the more we strive to obtain our own happiness and peace our own way. The less we are intentionally worshipping God, the more we begin worshipping the things of this world. We begin looking horizontal instead of vertical. Have you ever said or thought, "It would make everything better if I just had ___"? The Bible actually calls these heart idols. 1 John 5:21 (ESV) says, "Little children, keep yourself from idols." An idol is anything I want that has become more important than God. Famous theologian, John Calvin, actually calls our hearts little idol factories. This is true because our hearts were designed to worship, and if they are not worshipping God, then they are worshipping something else.

But, there is hope! Thank goodness we are not left there. My favorite phrase in all of Scripture begins one of the most hope-filled passages in the Bible. Ephesians 2:4-8 (ESV) states,

> *"But God, being rich in mercy, because of the great love with which He loved us, even when we were dead in our trespasses, made us alive together with Christ- by grace you have been saved- and raised us up with Him and seated us with Him in the heavenly places in Christ Jesus, so that in the coming ages He might show the immeasurable riches of His grace and kindness toward us in Christ Jesus. For by grace you have been saved through faith. And this is not your own doing: it is the gift of God."*

He loves you. Not because of anything you have done, but by grace alone. God sent His only Son to live a perfect life and take all of your sin upon Himself. He literally put our sin to *death* on the cross and then rose again to demonstrate that sin no longer has power over the lives of those who believe in His Name. The power of sin in your life was defeated, and there is hope. Hope to change. Hope to worship God, and in that, find deep enduring satisfaction at the heart level that nothing else can give. He saved you from enslavement to sin and the worship of idols. You are no longer enslaved. You are free to choose differently.

If this is true in your life, you have been "imputed with," or given, the righteousness of Jesus Christ. God sees you just as He sees Jesus, which is perfect and blameless. However, as long as we are here on this earth, it will be a battle to live like this because we are human, and there is still sin in our hearts.

In our daily repetition of the Gospel, we find the reason, hope, and power to worship God in all things. *The Gospel Primer*, by Milton Vincent, breaks these Gospel truths down succinctly and easily. Here are a few that the author lists.

1. Power of God - The Bible describes the Gospel as "the power of God." Nothing else in Scripture is ever described this way.

2. Armor of God - All of the pieces of the armor of God are just synonyms for the Gospel. It is your protection against evil.

3. My heart is satisfied, and I am transformed - The Gospel displays God's glory. When I reflect on it, it not only satisfies my heart's deepest longing, which is to see the glory of God, but it also begins to transform my heart.

4. I see God's love for me - When I train my heart to remember that if God loved me enough to sacrifice His Son's life for me, then He must be guided by that same love in His actions toward me.

5. I have all I need - 2 Peter 1:3 tells us that the Gospel contains all I need "for life and Godliness." He will supply all of my needs as long as I am abiding with Him there.

6. I see my freedom - Through the Gospel, I see that sin does not have power over me, and I am forgiven and seen by God as righteous. Therefore, my desire to sin is weakened, and it is here I find freedom from daily sin and daily guilt. Even when I have failed, God's grace toward me does not stop or change.

7. Understand love for others - Because of God's great and undeserved love toward me when I did not deserve it or earn it, I am compelled and motivated to love others at their best and at their worst. I am also called to forgive when I have been wronged because of the forgiveness I

have been shown when I did not deserve it. This is fueled by the power of grace in me. Even with the most difficult people, I am without excuse.

8. I learn that I decrease and He increases - Through the Gospel, I have been stripped of my pride, as I have done nothing to earn this favor, and I fail often. Joy flourishes where there is humility. Pride is at the root of all sin. The more I die to myself and my pride, the less I will sin, and the more my passion for God will thrive. In the Gospel, you will find true peace, both inner peace with God, and outward peace in life and relationships.

These are just some of the practical, daily implications of the Gospel. I think you will find that repeating these daily will make you more in awe of Him, which is the key to cultivating peace. You will not want to worship anything other than Him.

7.

Fighting Well

The Lord has been teaching me how to fight well. He will fight for us, but we have to do our part. He may want us to give up or sacrifice something that we love. He may just want us to desperately seek Him in faith. No matter which direction you find Him drawing you, fighting well requires action. I want to share two stories that show what it means to fight for your heart. Both of these stories mean a lot to me.

The first story is the story of Princess Amanda and the Dragon from *Tales of the Kingdom*, by David R. Mains and Karen Burton Mains. This is the story of a young princess, as we all are in the eyes of God. She lives in a place called Great Park, which is under the King's (Jesus') domain. In Great Park, certain things are forbidden for the safety of all who live there.

Amanda, like so many of the characters in *Tales of the Kingdom*, reminds us of ourselves. In this story, she is faced with a dilemma. She has been warned by Caretaker, who is the character much like the Holy Spirit, not to keep any dragon eggs that are present in the Spring, as it is forbidden.

One warm spring day, Amanda finds an egg and decides to keep it for a while instead of taking it to Caretaker's house to be disposed of. It is not long before a baby dragon cracks through the amber-colored shell, as cute as a dragon can appear. Amanda is torn. She knows what she is supposed to do, but she cannot resist playing with the little dragon for a while. Amanda ends up keeping the dragon for months. As it turns out, the cute creature becomes a demanding pet. All of Amanda's time is taken up with the care and feeding of the dragon. Amanda becomes so absorbed with her new love, that she starts to forget about her other relationships. She becomes more distant and defensive as people attempt to find out what has been occupying her time. Amanda does not stop caring for the dragon, nor does she confess her sin to others.

She does not notice at first, but the dragon's cuteness begins to wear off, and an ominous yellow glow appears in his eyes. The glow grows brighter with each passing day. Amanda used to laugh at the silly people who told her that dragons were dangerous, but now, she is starting to think they may have been right. When Amanda finally comes to her senses and realizes what she has done, she takes the dragon far away from her home and tells it to stay away from her and the people of the Kingdom. The dragon becomes very angry, and Amanda fully realizes that her cute pet has become a deadly monster. Her life, and the lives of all the residents of the Kingdom, are in danger. She cries out for Caretaker to come to rescue her. He appears, and she cries, "Kill it! Kill it!"

But He cannot.

Caretaker tells Amanda, "I cannot kill this dragon. Only the one who loves a forbidden thing can do the slaying. You will always hate me if I do it. Only you can slay this dragon." He gives Amanda an ax, and He stays close by while she fights her dragon. A fierce battle ensues, and with the coaching of Caretaker, Amanda slays her beast.

I can relate to Amanda. There have been times in my life that I did not listen to the Holy Spirit. My emotions caused me to rebel because I did not want to deny my own desires. These types of decisions only lead to despair and heartache, but there is hope. God gives us all the resources we need to fight well. He wants to protect us and help us. We must put on the full armor of God so we can see clearly and withstand temptations. The armor of God is listed out and described in the book of Ephesians.

> *"Finally, be strong in the Lord and in the strength of his might. Put on the whole armor of God, that you may be able to stand against the schemes of the devil. For we do not wrestle against flesh and blood, but against the rulers, against the authorities, against the cosmic powers over this present darkness, against the spiritual forces of evil in the heavenly places. Therefore take up the whole armor of God, that you may be able to withstand in the evil day, and having done all, to stand firm. Stand therefore, having fastened on the belt of truth, and having put on the breastplate of righteousness, and, as shoes for your feet, having put on the readiness given by the gospel of peace. In all circumstances take up the shield of faith, with which you can extinguish all the flaming darts of the evil one; and take the helmet of salvation,*

> *and the sword of the Spirit, which is the word of*
> *God, praying at all times in the Spirit, with all*
> *prayer and supplication. To that end, keep alert*
> *with all perseverance, making supplication for*
> *all the saints." (Ephesians 6:10-18, NIV)*

Another story that I love is the story of a courageous woman in Luke 8. When Jesus returned to Galilee from the country of Gerasenes, He found many people waiting on Him. Jesus was on His way to heal an important man's daughter. In the crowd, there was a woman who had heard of God's healing power. She had been bleeding for twelve years. Most likely, everyone in the town knew her and knew she was unclean. She was forbidden to associate with people, and no one was allowed to touch her. She had spent all of her money on doctors, without results, and was sentenced to a life of hiding in shame. She knew that Jesus could heal her, but she had to get close enough to touch Him without being seen. She was desperate. On hands and knees, she crawled her way through the crowd toward Jesus. She found an opening, and quickly thrusted her arm through dusty ankles and ran her fingers along the fringe of His garment.

He immediately stopped and said, "Who is the one who touched me?" Peter, with some irritation, said to Jesus, "Master, the crowds surround you and are pressing in on you!" But Jesus, still looking, said, "Someone touched me, for I perceive that power has gone out from me" (Matthew 9:20-22, Mark 5:25-34, Luke 8:43-48, NIV). Meekly the bleeding woman said, "It was me." She stepped toward Jesus, and the crowd parted. In tears, she dropped to her knees and said, "I touched you, Master." Jesus was clearly moved. He went toward her, wiped her tears, and said, "Daughter, your faith has made you well; go in peace." Her shame had kept her hidden, but she was willing to expose herself to fight, to claw her way through the dirt and shuffling feet of the crowd in order to get to the only Source of true power and healing. And then...rather than holding her healing close to her chest, she stood up and exposed herself in her blatant sin of disregarding Jewish law.

When this courageous woman reached out to touch Jesus, she did not just touch the fringe of His garment, but rather the *tzitzit*. These ritual tassels are placed on each corner of every four-corner garment. They are described in detail in the book of Numbers.

> "The Lord said to Moses, "Speak to the Israel-
> ites and say to them: 'Throughout the genera-
> tions to come you are to make tassels on the
> corners of your garments, with a blue cord on
> each tassel. You will have these tassels to look
> at and so you will remember all the commands
> of the Lord, that you may obey them and not
> prostitute yourselves by chasing after the lusts
> of your own hearts and eyes. Then you will re-
> member to obey all my commands and will be
> consecrated to your God. I am the Lord your
> God, who brought you out of Egypt to be your
> God. I am the Lord your God.'" (Numbers 15:37-
> 41, NIV)

The jewelry that I am able to create reminds me of the *tzitzit* on the Lord's garment. It is a symbolic reminder to me of the promises and commands He has laid out for us in His Word.

These stories show two ways of fighting for our faith. Sometimes, like Amanda, we have to pick up our sword and go fight for our freedom. Other times we must be broken and desperate enough to drag ourselves towards it. I have done and will continue to do both.

Throughout my life, I have had to fight for my free-dom. Freedom from the enemy and freedom from myself. I have had to pick up my sword and go to battle for my heart. Regardless of the path you take to freedom, the moments of that space are always uncomfortable. But, just like growing pains for a child, growth always occurs in moments of pain or discomfort. The good news is the Lord is always there for us in those uncomfortable moments giving us the grace we need to make it through—

Uncomfortable Grace.

BOOKS MENTIONED

Blackaby, Henry, Richard Blackaby, and Claude V. King. *Experiencing God Workbook: Knowing and Doing the Will of God, Updated*. Nashville, TN: Lifeway, 2007.

Cloud, Henry, and John Sims Townsend. *Boundaries*. Grand Rapids, MI: Zondervan, 2001.

Idleman, Kyle. *Grace Is Greater: God's Plan to Overcome Your Past, Redeem Your Pain, and Rewrite Your Story*. Grand Rapids, MI: Baker Books, a division of Baker Publishing Group, 2017.

Mains, David R., Zhivko Zhelev, and Karen Burton Mains. *Tales of the Kingdom*. Chicago, IL: Mainstay Ministries, 1983.

Omartian, Stormie. *The Power of a Praying Wife*. Eugene, OR: Harvest House Publishers, 2017.

Phillips, Nathan, and Jane Phillips. *Relationships: 33 Tools to Help You Navigate Them Well*. Lifebooks, 2011.

Sorrow, Abigail. *Full*. Charleston: Createspace Independent Publishing, 2018.

Tripp, Paul David. *Instruments in the Redeemer's Hand: People in Need of Change Helping People in Need of Change*. Phillipsburg, NJ: P&R Publishing Company, 2002.

Vincent, Milton. *A Gospel Primer: for Christians*. Bemidji, MN: Focus Publishing, 2008.

Vischer, Phil. *Sidney & Norman: A Tale of Two Pigs*. Nashville, TN: Thomas Nelson, 2012.

My Story Isn't Over...

Made in the USA
Columbia, SC
04 October 2020